FROM GRACE TO GRACE

A PRAYER AND HEALING JOURNAL

FROM GRACE TO GRACE

A PRAYER AND HEALING JOURNAL

SIMONE OLIVER

TRUSTED BOOKS
A DIVISION OF DEEP RIVER BOOKS

2nd Printing 2014.

Trusted Books is an imprint of Deep River Books. The views expressed or implied in this work are those of the author. To learn more about Deep River Books, go online to www.DeepRiverBooks.com.

ISBN 13: 978-1-63269-241-2
Library of Congress Catalog Card Number: 2012922104

Contents

Acknowledgments

I thank my husband, Allen, whose unfailing faith in God and unconditional love for me have made him the wind beneath my wings.

I thank all of my family and my friends who were with me throughout my recovery and have remained so.

And to the phenomenal women at Princeton Theological Seminary who are a continual source of invaluable support and inspiration and the sisters of Delta Sigma Theta, Inc., thank you for your constant prayers.

PREFACE
The Healing Journey Begins

Life has taught me that pain is an all-encompassing, cosmic experience. Whether you've lost a loved one to death or to another, been betrayed, endured the heartache of divorce, or been victimized or preyed upon, affliction is part and parcel of the human experience.

How do you respond when the unthinkable happens? After being stalked for several months, I was savagely attacked, stabbed over thirty times, and left for dead four days prior to my wedding date. The major artery in my neck was severed, and my lungs and kidneys were punctured. After I was found and rushed to the emergency room, the hands of three skilled physicians operated simultaneously as the hand of the Great Physician directed death to flee.

I woke out of a coma on the morning of the third day after the attack. I soon discovered I had suffered a spinal cord injury, and in addition to needing to recover from my stab and surgical wounds, I was diagnosed as a paraplegic.

The injuries I suffered came from the hands of my "pastor," the "shepherd of my soul." And I had to make a choice in the midst of the unthinkable. I chose to respond with the belief that God had not forsaken me and that God had a plan for my life. I chose to respond with forgiveness, and I chose to respond to God's love. I believe that you can too.

After eight months of intensive rehabilitation therapy, I learned to walk again—with a limp, with a cane, and with a lack of normal sensation. But I am walking nevertheless. I am walking in love, I am walking in joy, and I am walking in freedom. I now know the meaning of "the joy of the Lord is your strength" (Neh. 8:10, KJV). I encourage you to add some fight to your faith. God has a plan for your life! Your grief, pain, and despair are temporary—if you will allow them to be. You have a choice to make about how you heal: you can be bitter or better; you can be stifled or become strong. God can take you from grace to grace.

I encourage you to embrace your brokenness and open a space in your heart for God's unconditional and healing love to abide. These pages are designed for quiet reflections and responses. It is my hope that you, by meditating on these Scripture passages and inspirational quotes, while spending some time in self-reflection, will allow God to meet you in your pain and then follow Him on *your* journey to healing.

> Bless the LORD, O my soul, And forget not all His benefits: Who forgives all your iniquities, Who heals all your diseases, Who redeems your life from destruction, Who crowns you with lovingkindness and tender mercies, Who satisfies your mouth with good things, So that your youth is renewed like the eagle's.
>
> -Psalm 103:2-5

A Prayer of Yearning

Holy One, I pray that You will ignite my heart with the fire of Your love. Set ablaze in me laughter so deep and rich—a laughter that delights in who You are. Let me dance with You. Let my feet gently rest upon Yours as You swing me and swirl me to the rhythm of Your perfect will and purpose. Let me see You in the beauty of Your holiness from this ash heap of my life. Let me fully embrace my brokenness, disappointments, and adversities, and by taking them into my arms and bringing all of the fragments into Your presence, may I find joy in my lamenting.

~ S. Oliver

Have mercy on me, O Lord, for I am weak;
O Lord, heal me, for my bones are troubled.

~Psalm 6:2

Reflections

I'm here. I love you…
There is nothing you can ever do to lose my love…

I am stronger than Depression and I am braver than
Lonliness and nothing will ever exhaust me.

-Elizabeth Gilbert
Eat, Pray, Love

Reflections

As one whom his mother comforts, So I will comfort you;
And you shall be comforted in Jerusalem.

~Isaiah 66:13

Reflections

And I felt like my heart had been so thoroughly and irreparably broken that there could be no real joy again… Everyone wanted me to pick up the pieces and move on, but I had to lie in the mud with my arms wrapped around myself, grieving, until I didn't have to anymore.

-Anne Lamott
Operating Instructions: A Journal of My Son's First Year

Reflections

But Jesus turning and seeing her said, Daughter, be of good cheer; thy faith hath made thee whole. And the woman was made whole from that hour.

~Matthew 9:22 ASV

Reflections

Scars are not injuries. A scar is a healing.
After injury, a scar is what makes you whole.

-China Mieville
The Scar

Reflections

There is therefore now no condemnation
to them that are in Christ Jesus.

~Romans 8:1 ASV

Reflections

Shame, blame, disrespect, betrayal, and the withholding of affection damage the roots from which love grows. Love can only survive these injuries if they are acknowledged, healed and rare.

-Brene Brown
The Gifts of Imperfection: Let Go of Who You Think You're Supposed to Be and Embrace Who You Are

Reflections

Therefore I despise myself and repent in dust and ashes.

~Job 42:6 NIV

Reflections

Shame is a soul eating emotion.

-C. G. Jung

Reflections

What then are we to say about these things?
If God is for us, who is against us?

~Romans 8:31 HCSB

Reflections

Do I have YOUR permission to be a Supernatural God?
If I want to open heaven, and in a moment in time, touch the heart of a daughter and supernaturally break all the darkness, shame, and torment in her life, MAY I DO THAT?

~Jim Anderson
Unmasked: Exposing the Cultural Sexual Assault

Reflections

But the eyes of the LORD are on those who fear him,
on those whose hope is in his unfailing love,
to deliver them from death and keep them alive in famine.

~Psalm 33:18–19 NIV

Reflections

If you're reading this … Congratulations, you're alive.
If that's not something to smile about,
then I don't know what is.

-Chad Sugg
Monsters Under Your Head

Reflections

Blessed be the God and Father of our Lord Jesus Christ,
who according to his great mercy begat us again unto a living
hope by the resurrection of Jesus Christ from the dead,

~1 Peter 1:3 ASV

Reflections

We must accept finite disappointment,
but never lose infinite hope.

~Martin Luther King, Jr.

Reflections

Where then is my hope? As for my hope, who can see it?

~Job 17:15

Reflections

I want to believe that life isn't full of darkness.
Even if storms come to pass, the sun will shine again.
No matter how painful and
hard the rain may beat down on me.

~Natsuki Takaya

Reflections

Don't panic. I'm with you. There's no need to fear for I'm
your God. I'll give you strength. I'll help you.
I'll hold you steady, keep a firm grip on you.

~Isaiah 41:10 MSG

Reflections

Our deepest fear is not that we are inadequate.
Our deepest fear is that we are powerful beyond measure…
We were born to manifest the glory of God within us.
It's not just in some of us; it's in everyone.

~Marianne Williamson
Return to Love: Reflections on Principals of "A Course in Miracles"

Reflections

Peace I leave with you, My peace I give to you;
not as the world gives do I give to you.
Let not your heart be troubled, neither let it be afraid.

~John 14:27

Reflections

Here is the world. Beautiful and terrible things will happen.
Don't be afraid.

~Frederick Buechner
Beyond Words: Daily Readings in the ABC's of Faith

Reflections

The Lord is the One who will go before you.
He will be with you; He will not leave you or forsake you.
Do not be afraid or discouraged.

~Deuteronomy 31:8 HCSB

Reflections

Our greatest fear should not be of failure but of succeeding at things in life that don't really matter.

~Frances Chan
Crazy Love:
Overwhelmed by a Relentless God

Reflections

A Prayer of Expectancy

Lord, I come to You with expectancy. What I am expecting though, I'm not quite sure. You have surprised me so many times before. I expect that You will hear and answer my prayers in some odd way. I expect that my fears will subside when I choose to confront them with You gently leading the way. I expect some evidence of Your love in the accidental smile of a stranger, a sudden melody in my heart, or the unforeseen call from a friend. I expect that all my broken pieces will be fused together by breath and spirit.

I am saddened to realize that You cannot expect much in return from me. I say yes and do no. I say I will but then I don't. I cry when I laugh and laugh when I am angry. O God, I'm a mess! That is why I come to You with expectancy because I know in some odd way You will give me what I need when I need it.

~S. Oliver

He replied, "You of little faith, why are you so afraid?"
Then he got up and rebuked the winds and the waves,
and it was completely calm.

~Matthew 8:26 NIV

Reflections

Faith is not the belief that God will do what you want.
It is the belief that God will do what is right.

~Max Lucado
He Still Moves Stones

Reflections

The simple truth is that if you had a mere kernel of faith,
a poppy seed, say, you would tell this mountain,
"Move!" and it would move.
There is nothing you wouldn't be able to tackle.

~Matthew 17:20 MSG

Reflections

The reason birds can fly and we can't is simply because they have perfect faith, for to have faith is to have wings.

-J.M. Barrie
The Little White Bird

Reflections

So Jesus answered and said to them, "Have faith in God."

-Mark 11:22

Reflections

Faith consists in believing when it is beyond
the power of reason to believe.

~Voltaire

Reflections

Don't fret or worry. Instead of worrying, pray.
Let petitions and praises shape your worries into prayers,
letting God know your concerns.

~Philippians 4:6 MSG

Reflections

The more you pray, the less you'll panic.
The more you worship, the less you worry.

-Rick Warren
The Purpose of Christmas

Reflections

Therefore do not worry about tomorrow,
for tomorrow will worry about itself.
Each day has enough trouble of its own.

~Matthew 6:34 NIV

Reflections

Worry doesn't empty tomorrow of its sorrow,
it empties today of its strength.

-Corrie Ten Boom

Reflections

You will not fear the terror of the night,
the arrow that flies by day,

~Psalm 91:5 HCSB

Reflections

Anxious people can have a hard time staying motivated,
period, because their intense focus on worries
distracts them from their goals.

~Winifred Gallagher
Rapt: Attention and the Focused Life

Reflections

Trust in the Lord with all your heart,
and lean not on your own understanding;
In all your ways acknowledge Him,
and He shall direct your paths.

~Proverbs 3:5–6

Reflections

The best way to find out
if you can trust somebody is to trust them.

~Ernest Hemingway

Reflections

You will keep him in perfect peace,
Whose mind is stayed on You, Because he trusts in You.

~Isaiah 26:3

Reflections

Trust is the fruit of a relationship
in which you know you are loved.

-W. Paul Young

Reflections

Trust in the Lord, and do good; Dwell in the land,
and feed on His faithfulness.

~Psalm 37:3

Reflections

Never be afraid to trust an unknown future to a known God.

-Corrie Ten Boom

Reflections

Jesus prayed, "Father, forgive them;
they don't know what they're doing."

~Luke 23:34 MSG

Reflections

People are often unreasonable, irrational, and self-centered.
Forgive them anyway…

In the final analysis, it is between you and God.
It was never between you and them anyway.

~Mother Teresa

Reflections

If we confess our sins, He is faithful and righteous to forgive
us our sins and to cleanse us from all unrighteousness.

~1 John 1:9 HCSB

Reflections

To be a Christian means to forgive the inexcusable because God has forgiven the inexcusable in you.

~C.S. Lewis

Reflections

For thou, Lord, art good, and ready to forgive,
And abundant in lovingkindness unto all them
that call upon thee.

~Psalm 86:5 ASV

Reflections

Forgiveness is the fragrance that the violet sheds on the heel that has crushed it.

-Mark Twain

Reflections

Yet in all these things we are more than conquerors
through Him who loved us.

~Romans 8:37

Reflections

In the depth of winter, I finally learned that within me
there lay an invincible summer.

-Albert Camus

Reflections

But those who wait on God get fresh strength.
They spread their wings and soar like eagles,
They run and don't get tired, they walk and don't lag behind.

~Isaiah 40:31 MSG

Reflections

Courage isn't having the strength to go on—it is going on when you don't have strength.

-Napoleon Bonaparte

Reflections

Jehovah is my light and my salvation; Whom shall I fear?
Jehovah is the strength of my life; Of whom shall I be afraid?

~Psalm 27:1 ASV

Reflections

Spending time with God is the key to our strength and success in all areas of life.

~Joyce Meyer

Reflections

And the peace of God, which transcends all understanding,
will guard your hearts and your minds in Christ Jesus.

~Philippians 4:7 NIV

Reflections

Peace is the only battle worth waging.

~Albert Camus

Reflections

Let him turn away from evil and do good;
Let him seek peace and pursue it.

~1 Peter 3:11

Reflections

An eye for an eye will only make the whole world blind.

-Mahatma Gandhi
The Story of My Experiments with Truth

Reflections

Therefore, having been justified by faith,
we have peace with God through our Lord Jesus Christ.

~Romans 5:1

Reflections

Peace is always beautiful.

~Walt Whitman
Leaves of Grass

Reflections

A Prayer of Thanksgiving

Holy One, I thank You that You do not despise my anger. I thank You that You do not disregard my rantings of frustration. I thank You that You do not disengage from my desperate cursings. For You are still the High Priest, touched by the feelings of all of my infirmities, for even my thoughts are my prayers.

~S. Oliver

The God of old is your dwelling place,
and underneath are the everlasting arms.
He drives out the enemy before you and
commands, "Destroy!"

~Deuteronomy 33:27 HCSB

Reflections

The means by which we achieve victory are as important as the victory itself.

~Brandon Sanderson
The Way of Kings

Reflections

Do not fear, for I am with you; do not be afraid,
for I am your God.
I will strengthen you; I will help you;
I will hold on to you with My righteous right hand.

~Isaiah 41:10 HCSB

Reflections

The fight isn't over until you win.

-Robin Hobb
Royal Assassin

Reflections

But thanks be to God, who giveth us the victory
through our Lord Jesus Christ.

~1 Corinthians 15:57 ASV

Reflections

I am not a victim. No matter what I've been through,
I'm still here.
I have a history of victory.

-Steve Maraboli

Reflections

Don't bother your head with braggarts or wish you could succeed like the wicked.

~Psalm 37:1 MSG

Reflections

Envy is the art of counting the other fellow's blessings instead of your own.

~Harold G. Coffin

Reflections

Do not let your heart envy sinners,
but always be zealous for the fear of the Lord.

–Proverbs 23:17 NIV

Reflections

Envy is the religion of the mediocre. It comforts them,
it soothes their worries, and finally it rots their souls.

~Carlos Ruiz Zafon
The Angel's Game

Reflections

Don't envy a violent man or choose any of his ways.

~Proverbs 3:31 HCSB

Reflections

Any intelligent fool can make things bigger,
more complex, and more violent.
It takes a touch of genius—and a lot of courage
to move in the opposite direction.

-E.F. Schumacher

Reflections

A merry heart does good, like medicine,
But a broken spirit dries the bones.

~Proverbs 17:22

Reflections

The greater part of our happiness or misery depends upon our dispositions, and not our circumstances.

~Martha Washington

Reflections

Satisfy us in the morning with Your faithful love
so that we may shout with joy and be glad all our days.

~Psalm 90:14 HCSB

Reflections

Christian contentment is that sweet, inward, quiet, gracious frame of spirit, which freely submits to and delights in God's wise and fatherly disposal in every condition.

-Jeremiah Burroughs

Reflections

So I take pleasure in weaknesses, insults, catastrophes, persecutions, and in pressures, because of Christ. For when I am weak, then I am strong.

~2 Corinthians 12:10 HCSB

Reflections

Learn to value yourself, which means:
fight for your happiness.

~Ayn Rand

Reflections

A Prayer of Praise

Holy God, I have some pain, and trauma, and disappointment to work out, but I thank You for allowing me to embrace the journey; it is by Your grace alone. The journey leads me into Your presence. The journey leads me into Your love. The journey leads me into parts of me that I wish could be forgotten. Sometimes I am led into fear and anxiety. Sometimes I am led into pain and despair. For I have walked through the valley of the shadow of death and yet, even while surrounded by evil, You were with me.

It is You, Great God, that makes my heart sing. It is You that causes me to smile in the midst of pain and makes my spirit alive with anticipation because I believe that I will see the goodness of the Lord in the land of the living. So with humble praise and adoration, I magnify Your name. I exalt You O God, for there is none like You! O God of many names, I call You Faithful, Just, and True.

My gift to You is the broken pieces and the fragments of my life. As I have been broken, so let me be given.

~S. Oliver

Finally, brethren, whatsoever things are true, whatsoever things are honorable, whatsoever things are just, whatsoever things are pure, whatsoever things are lovely, whatsoever things are of good report; if there be any virtue, and if there be any praise, think on these things.

~Philippians 4:8 ASV

Reflections

Your battles inspired me—not the obvious material battles but those that were fought and won behind your forehead.

-James Joyce

Reflections

Praise be to the Lord, to God our Savior,
who daily bears our burdens.

~Psalm 68:19 NIV

Reflections

You wanna fly, you got to give up the [stuff]
that weighs you down.

-Toni Morrison
Song of Solomon

Reflections

The Lord is good, a strong hold in the day of trouble;
and he knoweth them that trust in him.

~Nahum 1:7 KJV

Reflections

Victories are won while on your knees!
Keep praying for those who rise up against you.
Fear not. The Lord has rectified the problem.
Prayer is POWERFUL!

~Anita R. Sneed-Carter

Reflections

At Piece

surrounded by the shadows
I have given myself over to Your love.
absurd, that I found You
wounded and suffering.
held captive by Christ
I contemplate my own agony.
is suffering really redemptive?
I try to find respite
in the fragments
of my brokenness,
in every shard.
I can never be the same, you know.
graciously,
I make peace with my pieces
and in them
I am blessed.

-S. Oliver

In the end, it's not *what* you go through
but *how* you go through
that tells the world who you are.

~S. Oliver

RESOLUTION

if I do not trust
i cannot be betrayed.
if I do not love
i cannot be hurt.
if I do not care
i cannot be disappointed.
but
trusting, loving, and caring
bring me joy
and
are a few of the good things
life is made of.
so I will continue to risk betrayal
i will continue to risk pain
i will continue to risk disappointment
that I may fully live.

~S. Oliver

A Special Invitation

I realize that you may have worked through this journal without having a personal relationship with Jesus Christ. You may attend a church or maybe you don't. Either way, I invite you to enter into the love of God through Jesus Christ.

This is the simple gospel: Because of one man's sin, we are all born into sin and under condemnation (Romans 5:12). Sin separates humankind from God. The consequence of sin is both physical and spiritual death. God, in His grace, has made a way for human beings to be reconciled to Him. He sent His only Son, Jesus Christ, to earth. And He, by dying on the cross as a substitute for sinners and rising from the dead, provided the only way for those who repent to be forgiven of their sins (John 14:6). Jesus is alive (Mark 16:19) and offers us spiritual life and a new relationship with God. Acts 16:31 says, "Believe on the Lord Jesus Christ, and you will be saved."

Here are the steps everyone must take in order to experience salvation:

- Realize that the penalty for sin is eternal death (Romans 6:23a).
- Admit that you are a sinner (Romans 3:23).
- Acknowledge that there is nothing you can do to save yourself (Romans 3:20).

- Realize that Jesus Christ has paid the penalty for sin (Romans 5:8–9).
- Repent of (turn from) your sin (Luke 13:3).
- Believe in (turn to) Jesus Christ alone for salvation (Romans 10:9), and accept Him as your Lord and Savior.

You can pray a simple prayer in the privacy of your home, in the privacy of your own soul, and know that God has forgiven you and you are saved.

You now have the opportunity to enter into a loving, life-giving relationship with the God of the universe. In addition to spending time with Him in private, I encourage you to find fellowship in a biblically sound, safe church where you can continue to grow in the grace and knowledge of God.

Peace and blessings,
Simone Oliver

ENDNOTES

1. All literary quotations are from "Popular Quotes," Good Reads, last accessed Dec. 6, 2012, https://www.goodreads.com/quotes.

CPSIA information can be obtained
at www.ICGtesting.com
Printed in the USA
BVOW03s1024091217
502390BV00001B/71/P

9 781632 692412